W9-CYA-125

The Ballad of
THE PENGUIN OF DEATH
Method 412

for David

ISBN-13: 978-0-7407-7383-9
ISBN-10: 0-7407-7383-6

08 09 10 11 12 SDB 10 9 8 7 6 5 4 3 2 1

www.edwardmonkton.com

www.andrewsmcmeel.com

The Ballad of
THE PENGUIN OF DEATH
Method 412

Edward Monkton

Andrews McMeel
Publishing, LLC
Kansas City

The Penguin softly calls you
From his palace in the snow.
Though every sinew holds you back
You know that YOU MUST GO.

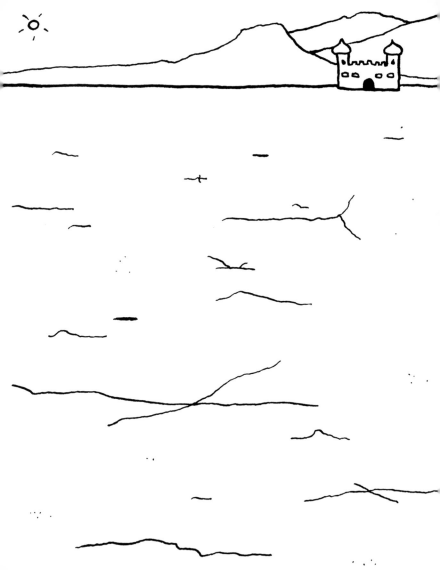

And when you've made the journey
'cross the BARREN icy land,
The Penguin simply nods and says,
"I knew you'd UNDERSTAND.

"I knew that you would come, my friend,
Now won't you follow me?
I've made us both some BISCUITS
And a warming pot of tea."

You step inside his palace
And you GASP with silent awe
At the shining crystal ceiling
And the glowing crystal floor.

"Sit down, my FRIEND," the Penguin says
And shows you to your seat,
Then he gently takes your boots off
And starts MASSAGING your feet.

He looks you in the eye and says,
"I know what I must do.
You've come for me to end your life
By METHOD 4-1-2."

"I have," you say, "dear Penguin,
I have come for my RELEASE.
And I'm mindful that this method
Is your final masterpiece."

The Penguin strokes your forehead
And he whispers "Very Well!"
Then he stands awhile in silence
And his CHEST begins to swell.

Then suddenly you hear it
In a voice so clear and strong,
A strange and SUBTLE melody
A HAUNTING Penguin song.

The words sink deep inside you
And they lift you from your chair.
Their POETRY and WISDOM
Leave you weightless in the air.

And each word is more BEAUTIFUL
And each note is more clear.
It's as though a HONEYED bell of truth
Is ringing in your ear.

You're a child of the forest,
You're a baby in the WOMB,
You're the Ruler of the Ancients
In your SACRED golden tomb.

"Oh, Penguin, won't you tell me
What enchantment, please, is this?
What manner of salvation?
What strange, euphoric BLISS?

"I'm a running mountain river,
I'm a brooding stormy sea!
Was there something in those BISCUITS?
Was there something in that TEA?"

Then, as you watch in helplessness,
This strange and SOULFUL bird
Throws his flippers heavenward
And sings ONE FINAL WORD.

A word so soft and HOLY
Yet so full of DREAD and pain,
A word that no one's sung before
And no one will again.

It melts into your consciousness
And ECHOES through your heart.
Its BEAUTY and its CRUELTY
Are tearing you apart.

Then tears of JOY start flowing
Like the Penguin knew they would
As, for the first time in your life,
You feel COMPLETELY UNDERSTOOD.

And you know the Penguin LOVES you
As what needs to happen must . . .

... You suddenly EXPLODE
Into a million specks of dust.

And out there in the ether
You are HAPPY. You are FREE.
The Penguin simply smiles
And pours another cup of tea.